Lydia Fotheringham is a partner of Anderson Beaton Lamond Solicitors in Perth where she maintains a strong base of farming clients. A solicitor with 25 years' experience, she is accredited by the Law Society of Scotland as a Specialist in Agricultural Law. Lydia is described in Chambers 2020 as "*pragmatic and sensible in her approach.*"

A Practical Introduction to Drafting Wills for Farmers in Scotland

A Practical Introduction to Drafting Wills for Farmers in Scotland

Lydia Fotheringham

Law Brief Publishing

Published 2022 by Law Brief Publishing, an imprint of Law Brief Publishing Ltd
30 The Parks
Minehead
Somerset
TA24 8BT

www.lawbriefpublishing.com

Paperback: 978-1-914608-22-3

This book is dedicated to Alan and Archie without whose love and support it would not have been possible.

PREFACE

Failure to plan for succession is often cited as one of the biggest challenges facing the agricultural community in Scotland.

This practical guide is an introduction to drafting wills for farmers in Scotland. It covers the main issues which arise in practice and should be of interest to solicitors working in agricultural law who wish to learn more about will drafting, solicitors dealing with private client work who wish to learn more about the specifics of drafting wills for farmers and generally anyone with an interest in succession planning for farmers.

I would like to thank my father Andrew Arbuckle and my colleague Kirsty Dutch for reading chapters of this book in draft. Thanks also to Tim Kevan and Garry Wright at Law Brief Publishing for suggesting the book in the first place, helping me through the writing process and publishing the book.

The law stated in this book is believed to be correct and up to date as at 30th June 2022.

Lydia Fotheringham
July 2022

CONTENTS

CHAPTER ONE

INTRODUCTION

Succession planning is hugely important to farming families but much of what is written on the subject is in general terms.

I believe there is merit in starting to look at succession planning by dealing first with the farmer's will because that allows the framework of rules on succession, partnership law and tax to impose order on the situation. The farmer can then decide not only how to provide for his or her family in the will, but may also be prompted to consider lifetime giving.

Most farmers have the same objectives when it comes to making a will. They want to see the farming business continued by future generations while at the same time providing for their spouse and any non-farming children.

The early chapters of this book explain how to take instructions from a farmer on the structure of their will and identify their specific assets which should be covered by the will. I highlight potential areas where the existing law may conflict with the farmer's wishes or instructions, for example legal rights and partnership law.

The later chapters of this book provide suggestions for active planning for succession both in utilising tax reliefs available and providing for non-farming children.

This book is intended for anyone advising farming clients who are owner occupiers or tenant farmers (or both) of small to medium sized units. These kinds or farmers are usually trading as sole traders or within a partnership or family company.

Drafting wills is an art not a science. This book can suggest common themes and pitfalls but ultimately every situation is unique.

Providing advice to owners of large estates and detailed inheritance tax advice are beyond the scope of this book.

CHAPTER TWO

INTESTACY

It is worth considering how the law of intestacy affects farmers, if for no other reason than to persuade a farmer that they must make a will.

The detail of the law of intestacy is beyond the scope of this book, but solicitors will all be aware that a surviving spouse or civil partner is entitled to Prior Rights on the estate of someone who dies without a will.

A Prior Rights claim comprises the residential dwellinghouse where the couple lived together to a maximum value of £473,000, the furniture and furnishings in the residential dwellinghouse and a cash sum of £89,000 reduced to £50,000 if the deceased had children.

Consider however the situation where the deceased is a farmer who does not own a residential dwellinghouse. This could be because the house is owned by a partnership or company or because the farm is leased.

The surviving spouse has no entitlement to the house and would be left with only the furniture and furnishings and cash sum.

Most people would prefer to provide more security for a spouse or civil partner and that can be achieved in a properly drafted will.

After Prior Rights the deceased's estate would be split among the Legal Rights claimants – spouse or civil partner and children – and beneficiaries of free estate – children or close family members.

Children who are involved in the farming enterprise and those who are not so involved would be treated equally. Likewise, children from any previous relationships would be treated equally with those from the current relationship.

If the farmer is cohabiting with someone they are not married to or in civil partnership with and the farmer dies intestate, the cohabitant may pursue a claim under the Family Law (Scotland) Act 2006 for provision from the deceased's estate on death. The result of such a claim is uncertain for the cohabitant and both the cohabitant and the executors would be involved in expensive court proceedings. Clear provision for the cohabitant in a will would avoid the uncertainty and expense of court proceedings.

In many cases the need to pay out cash or transfer assets to meet the claims of a cohabitant, Prior Rights, Legal Rights and the claims of beneficiaries entitled to the free estate may compromise the future viability of the farming business.

The following examples illustrate the problem:-

> *Alastair is a tenant farm and sole trader. He owns a residential property which is rented out. He has a small savings account. Alastair is married to Belinda and they have three adult children Chrissie, Della and Edward. Alastair dies suddenly without leaving a will. Edward, who works on the farm, is nominated by the executor dative to take over the tenancy. The remainder of the estate comprises the sole trader business valued at £50,000, the residential property valued at £150,000 and the savings of £9,000. Alastair's estate is distributed under the laws of intestacy as follows –*

Belinda – prior rights	*£50,000.00 (cash sum)*
Belinda – legal rights	*£3,000.00 (one third of moveable estate)*
Total –	*£53,000.00*
Chrissie, Della and Edward – legal rights	*£3,000 (one third of moveable estate – £1,000 each)*
Chrissie, Della and Edward – free estate	*£153,000 (residential property plus balance of savings – £51,000 each)*
Total each child	*£52,000*

Belinda cannot claim her prior rights over the residential property as she and Alastair did not live there together at the time of his death. The farmhouse is part of the farm tenancy which has passed to Edward. Belinda is left with £53,000. Although Edward acquires the farm tenancy, the business assets owned by his father as a sole trader may require to be sold to meet the prior rights and legal rights claims of the rest of the family.

If Alastair had made a will, he could have bequeathed the residential property to Belinda and the sole trader business assets to Edward. He could have provided for Chrissie and Della either by leaving the residential property in liferent to Belinda and in fee to his daughters or by taking out life insurance.

Tom is a farmer. The farm belongs to a trading company ABC Ltd. Tom is a director of ABC Ltd and owns 100% of the shares in that company. Tom is married to Susan and they have two young children Ursula and Victor. Tom was married before and has two adult children Freddie and Gertrude from that earlier marriage. Susan works with Tom in the farming business and is a director of ABC Ltd. Freddie also works with his father in the farming business and is a director of ABC Ltd. Gertrude is estranged from her father. Ursula and Victor are still at primary school. Tom dies suddenly with no will. The company is valued at date of death at £5,000,000. Tom also has a share portfolio worth £270,000 and a collection of classic tractors worth a surprising £150,000. His estate is entirely comprised of moveable property and totals £5,420,000. His estate is distributed according to the laws of intestacy as follows:-

Susan Prior Rights	*£50,000 (cash sum)*
Susan Legal Rights	*£1,790,000 (one third of moveable estate)*
Susan total	*£1,840,000*
Children legal rights	*£1,790,000 (one third of moveable estate)*
Children free estate	*£1,790,000 (one third of moveable estate)*

Children Total	*£3,580,000*
Ursula, Victor, Freddie and Gertrude each receive	*£1,193,333*

Again, Susan cannot claim her prior rights against the farmhouse because it belongs to ABC Ltd although she is in a much better position financially than Belinda in the example above. Freddie works in the farming business but he receives exactly the same inheritance as Gertrude, Ursula and Victor. A well drafted will could have provided for Susan, Freddie, Ursula and Victor appropriately and reduced Gertrude's share, albeit that she could still have claimed her legal rights.

> *Vera and Wilma are civil partners. They have no children. Vera owns a farm. Vera and Wilma farm in partnership. Vera dies suddenly without making a will. Apart from Wilma, Vera's only relative is her brother Bryan who lives in New Zealand and with whom she has had no contact in the last five years. Her estate at the date of her death comprises the farm valued at £800,000 (farmhouse worth £175,000), her capital balance in the partnership of £150,000 and £25,000 in a savings account. Vera's estate is distributed as follows:-*

Wilma prior rights	*£175,000 (value of the farmhouse)* *£89,000 (cash sum)*
Wilma legal rights	*£87,500 (one half of moveable assets after prior rights)*
Wilma total	*£351,500*
Bryan – free estate	*£625,000 (value of the farm under deduction of the farmhouse)* *£87,500 (balance of moveable assets after prior rights and legal rights)*
Bryan total	*£712,500*

In this example at least Wilma can claim the farmhouse but it is unlikely the eventual distribution was in line with Vera's wishes. Wilma and Bryan could enter into a Deed of Variation of Vera's will but that would require Bryan's consent as his entitlement would be affected.

Farmers, rich or poor, who do not have properly drafted wills risk causing financial and emotional problems for their families.

CHAPTER THREE

IDENTIFYING PROBLEM AREAS

Why is drafting a will for a farmer so difficult? There are a number of specific issues which particularly affect farmers and it is important to be able to identify and then attempt to deal with these in the farmer's will.

Issues to identify include:-

- Wealth – although the Inheritance Tax Regime favours farmers, they are usually high net worth individuals and it cannot be assumed that all of their assets qualify for tax relief on death.

- Business – there will be some form of business structure to be dealt with in the will.

- Legal Rights – the business structure will involve at least some element of moveable property meaning the estate is potentially vulnerable to a Legal Rights claim.

- Tenancies – the farmer's assets might include the tenant's interest in one or more leases.

- Delayed Succession Planning – the combination of a favourable tax status and lack of private pension provision can mean that the farmer has delayed succession planning to the point where tax planning measures such as gifting assets as Potentially Exempt Transfers are less useful.

- Competing interests in the estate – many testators prioritise their spouse but farmers tend to want to balance the interest of the spouse with a child who is involved in the farming business. Historically farms passed from father to son and, although more farmers are more concerned now to equalise the interests of all of their children, that mindset still informs decision making to some extent.

- Lack of Communication – there is often an assumption that children of a farmer will want to continue farming. That assumption may not be challenged leading to the situation where a farmer worries about equalising his estate between his children when if fact none of them actually wants to carry on the farming business which could be sold on the farmer's death, or even before to provide a comfortable retirement for the farmer.

These issues often overlap. The wealth of the farmer is often tied up in one substantial asset leaving little available cash to provide for non-farming children which in turn can lead to a legal rights claim. A lack of communication can lead to delayed succession planning.

The use of a checklist, see Appendix 4, can be useful to highlight problem areas and ensure these are dealt with in the will.

It may seem obvious but the solicitor making a will for a farmer has to ask detailed and searching questions to ensure they fully understand the farmer's assets.

CHAPTER FOUR

PRELIMINARY INFORMATION

Before a solicitor starts to draft a will for a farmer, and possibly even before he or she meets the client to take instructions, some preliminary information should be checked.

As with all testators the farmer must have capacity to make a will.

The additional information required to make a will for a farmer depends on whether the client owns or leases the land and how the farmer trades, whether that is in partnership, as a sole trader or using a private company structure.

Capacity

Any testator in Scotland must be at least 12 years old and have testamentary capacity.

Capacity is defined by its negative, incapacity, in the Adults With Incapacity (Scotland) Act 2000.

"Incapable" means incapable of

- Acting; or
- Making decisions; or
- Communicating decisions; or

- Understanding decisions; or
- Retaining the memory of decisions,

In this context testamentary capacity also includes an understanding of the nature and extent of the estate to which the will relates and the potential claims on the estate by a spouse or civil partner and children.

Title Deeds

The solicitor drafting the will should ask to see the title deeds, or obtain a Legal Report, to confirm who owns the farm.

The farm may belong to the individual making the will alone or with others or may belong to a partnership or company in which the farmer has an interest.

If the farm is owned by several individuals the solicitor should check if there is a survivorship destination which predates the will and therefore overrides the terms of a bequest of the farm in the will.

It is important to note if ownership of the farm is held by the partners of a partnership as trustees for and on behalf of that partnership. That structure of ownership has implications for the claiming of Legal Rights, see Chapter 7. Ownership by partners may be explicit from the face of the title or less obvious, see the section below on partnership accounts.

Once the ownership of the farm has been ascertained, the solicitor will be able to deal appropriately with the farmer's interest in the will.

Leases

It is not uncommon for owner occupier farmers to lease land in addition to the owned land so the solicitor preparing the will should always check if land is leased as well as owned.

Leases could take the form of traditional 1991 Act tenancies, Limited Duration Tenancies, Modern Limited Duration Tenancies, Short Limited Duration Tenancies or Grazing Lets.

All leases in which the farmer has an interest as a tenant should be checked. Chapter 8 provides more detail on succession to tenancies.

The solicitor drafting the will requires to establish whether the tenancies are capable of bequest or if the wording of the lease excludes assignees and beneficiairies. Even if the wording of the lease excludes assignees and beneficiaries the tenancy will still fall within the farmer's estate and can be transferred by the executors even if the lease is not specifically bequeathed. There are good, practical reasons not make a specific bequest of a lease, see Chapter 8.

The farmer should also be asked if he or she is the Landlord of any tenanted property.

Partnership Agreement

If there is a Partnership Agreement then by definition it predates the will the solicitor is about to draft and where the will conflicts with the terms of the earlier Partnership Agreement then the Partnership Agreement is given priority.

The solicitor drafting the will should check whether the Partnership Agreement contains a clause to the effect that the partnership terminates on the death of one of the partners.

If so, the Partnership Agreement might need to be amended to provide for continuation post death.

Amendment might also be required (subject of course to the agreement of all the partners) if the farmer's instructions for the will conflict with the terms of the Partnership Agreement.

The Partnership Agreement will typically provide for what should happen on the death of one of the partners. The value of the deceased partner's interest in the partnership as represented by the sums at credit of his or her current and capital accounts, is usually to be paid to that partner's estate on an agreed basis.

It is important that the farmer understands the basis on which the value is paid out to his or her estate. Does the agreement provide for a revaluation of all assets on death or must "book value" be used?

The difference can be very significant if land is sitting in the accounts at a historic value or if implements have depreciated in the accounts but have held their value well in the real world.

The terms of the Partnership Agreement usually give the continuing partners time, five or ten years is typical, to pay out the share of the deceased partner and the agreement might provide that interest is payable in addition.

If the title deeds or the accounts show that the farmland is owned by the partnership the solicitor drafting the will needs to know whether the farmland is legally heritable or moveable so you can advise the farmer on potential legal rights claims.

How could the farmland ever be moveable?

S22 of the Partnership (Scotland) Act 1890 states:-

> *Where land or any heritable interest therein has become partnership property, it shall, unless the contrary intention appears, be treated as between the partners (including the representatives of a deceased partner), and also as between the heirs of a deceased partner and his executors or administrators, as personal or moveable and not real or heritable estate*

The effect of this clause is that heritable property owned by a partnership is treated as being moveable property and therefore subject to a legal rights claim, see below Chapter 7.

That rule can be disapplied if *"the contrary intention appears"*, ie if the parties demonstrably agree otherwise.

The Partnership Agreement or later amendment may contain a clause disapplying s22 and confirming that heritable property remains heritable. The accounts of the partnership then usually show a separate "heritable capital" account, see Appendix 3.

Accounts

If the farmer is trading in partnership with others the solicitor making the will should check the partnership accounts to see if the farm is shown on the balance sheet.

Regardless of how the title is held the farm may have become a partnership asset if it is shown in the accounts as such on the basis that the holder of the title is holding in a bare trust for the partnership. If that is the case you may find there is a declaration of trust or a partnership minute to the effect that title is being held by the individual for and on behalf of the partnership.

As mentioned above, ownership by the partnership through the accounts in this way has important consequences for Legal Rights, see chapter 7.

The accounts may show a separate "heritable capital" account for heritable property in an attempt to escape the consequences of s22 of the Partnership Act 1890. If that is the case you should check that there is evidence in the Partnership Agreement, any amendment of that agreement or the minutes of partnership meetings that the partners have agreed to disapply s22.

The accounts will also disclose how the profit of the partnership is being split among the partners. As a succession planning point the older generation should be drawing a smaller percentage of profit so their drawings reduce their capital balance while the younger generation draw a higher percentage of profit and increase their capital balance.

Company Information

If the farmer trades using a limited company you will need to know who are the directors, who are the shareholders and the extent of each shareholding.

You should also enquire whether there are any shareholders agreements and if so check their terms to establish whether the farmer's ability to bequeath their shares in their will is restricted by the terms of the agreement. There may for example be a provision that the shares must first be offered to other shareholders possibly at an agreed price.

Remember that if the company owns the farmland, the farmer may own shares in the company which are moveable assets not a heritable asset. Again, see Chapter 7 on Legal Rights.

Family Tree

The solicitor should ensure they have full details of the farmer's immediate family. Is the farmer married or in a civil partnership? Does the farmer have children? Explain that this includes children from any previous relationship. Have any children pre-deceased and if so are there any grandchildren who could have a Legal Rights claim?

It is useful to draw up a brief family tree as an aide memoire. As explained in later chapters, Legal Rights can have a huge impact on farming estates, so the solicitor must clearly explain to the testator which family members potentially have Legal Rights claims and how much those claims could be.

If the farmer is separated or divorced, check the terms of any separation agreement to ensure that future Legal Rights claims have been excluded.

Duty of Care

Solicitors have a duty of care to beneficiaries and potential beneficiaries to ensure that the testator's wishes are promptly and properly drafted into a will.

As a general rule, wills should be drafted and sent to the client within 10 days of the initial meeting with follow ups as required if the client does not respond. Clear file notes protect the solicitor against a claim that the will did not reflect the testator's wishes.

CHAPTER FIVE

STRUCTURE OF THE WILL AND DRAFTING

The structure of the will – appointment of executors, specific legacies and residue clause – is of course the same for farmers as for anyone else.

Chapter 6 deals in more detail with the appointment of executors.

This chapter deals with specific legacies commonly found in farming wills, the use of liferents and considerations when drafting residue clauses.

Drafting Specific Legacies

Farmers often refer to "the farm" without differentiating between the heritable property, the capital balance in the partnership accounts or the shares in the family company.

Having investigated all the preliminary points highlighted in Chapter 4 the solicitor drafting the will should be in a position to draft an appropriate specific legacy of "the farm", for example:-

- **Partnership interest** – *I direct my executors to make over to my daughter Arabella my whole interest of whatever kind in the firm of ABC Farmers, a partnership formed under the law of Scotland and having a place of business at Darklands Farm, Caldwell, in the County of Perth as it is presently constituted or as it may be constituted at the time of my death.*

- **Shares in Company** – *I direct my executors to make over all to my son Blair my shares and stock of whatever classes in ABC Famers Limited (Company number SC1234), having its registered office at Darklands Farm, Caldwell in the County of Perth or such other shares or stock as may represent the same at the time of my death as a result of any amalgamation takeover or reorganisation of this company as to which my executors shall be the sole judges.*

- **Sole trader business including heritable property** – *I direct my executors to make over to my daughter Clarissa the farm and lands of Darklands including the farm house and other farm buildings, free of all expenses at the time of my death, together with the whole stock (whether living or dead), crops (whether growing or harvested including timber standing or fallen), unexhausted manures, seeds, fertilizers and other farm stores, farm vehicles, machinery and implements, and all other corporeal moveables used in the business of farming and my rights in all Basic Payment Entitlements, premia, subsidies and quotas, all in so far as belonging to me at the time of my death.*

- **Heritable Property** – *I direct my executors to make over to my son Derek the farm and lands of Darklands, Caldwell, in the County of Perth including the farm house and other farm buildings, free of all expenses of transfer, heritable debts and securities, and other capital burdens affecting the farm at the time of my death.*

Chapter 8 provides more information about succession to tenancies but the following is a typical style for a legacy of a tenancy and sole trader business:-

> *I direct my executors to make over my interest in the tenancy of the farm and lands of Darklands to my daughter Eva free*

of all expenses of transfer, heritable debts and securities, and other capital burdens affecting my interest at the time of my death, together with the whole stock (whether living or dead), crops (whether growing or harvested, including timber, standing or fallen), unexhausted manures, seeds, fertilizers and other farm stores, farm vehicles, machinery and implements and all other corporeal moveables used in the business of farming, all Tenant's Fixtures and Fittings, my whole interest in the value of any Tenant's Improvements and my rights in and to all Basic Payment Entitlements, premia, subsidies and quotas, all in so far as belonging to me at the time of my death.

In many cases a farmer may choose not to leave a specific legacy of the tenancy in the will as the bequest triggers a very tight timescale twenty-one day timescale for intimation to the Landlord following the death of the tenant farmer.

The farmer might therefore prefer to allow the tenancy to fall into intestacy. If that is the case, the farmer might still want to let his executors know what his intentions were in connection with the tenancy so they can take these into account when selecting a successor.

In such a situation a declaration of wishes could be used in the will or in a separate letter.

Typical wording would be:-

Without making any specific bequest of my tenancy of Darklands Farm I express the wish that my executors consider transferring the said tenancy to my son Ferdinand

Liferents

Where farmer wants to prioritise leaving assets to a child who is farming in preference to a spouse or civil partner they might want to consider leaving that spouse or civil partner a liferent interest in some or all of the farming assets.

A farmer can only do that if they own the asset to be liferented in their own name. If, for example, the farm house belongs to the farming partnership or the limited company then a bequest of a liferent interest will be of no effect.

If the farmer does own the asset in their own name and a liferent is to be granted the following should be considered:-

- How is maintenance of the asset to be dealt with? Should the liferenter or the capital beneficiary be responsible for day to day maintenance? Should extra-ordinary repairs or improvements be treated differently?

- When should the liferent end? The terms of the will could dictate that as well as on the death of the liferenter the liferent terminates on their renouncing the liferent, re-marrying or entering into a civil partnership or permanently moving into a care home.

- Who are the capital beneficiaries? Substitute beneficiaries should be nominated in case an original beneficiary predeceases the liferenter.

A typical liferent clause would be:-

> *I direct my Trustees to hold the farmhouse owned by me at Darklands Farm in liferent for my wife/husband/civil partner but that on the following terms and conditions namely:-*

*(First) the said ** shall be responsible for maintaining the Property in at least as good condition as it is at the date of my death; for paying all outgoings of whatever nature in relation to the Property including without prejudice to that generality all maintenance, insurance, Council Tax or any tax levied in substitute therefor, telephone and utility bills and all others;*

*(Second) the liferent will terminate on the death of the said **; should he/she renounce the said liferent; or should he/she go into long term care to the reasonable satisfaction of my trustees;*

*On the failure, termination or renunciation in whole or in part of the foregoing liferent, I direct my Trustees to make over the said farmhouse to such of my children *** and any other children of mine as survive the date or dates of vesting equally among them if more than one. Should any of my children predecease any date of vesting leaving issue (including adopted issue) who survive that date, each member of a generation of issue of such predeceasing child shall share equally in the part of my estate, both original and accresced, which would have gone to its parent if in life. Vesting shall occur on the date or dates of failure, termination or renunciation of the liferent.*

A difficult example:-

James and Charlie are civil partners. James farms in partnership with his son John and daughter Jane. Charlie is not involved in the farming business. The farm, including the farm house where James and Charlie live, is owned by the partnership. James wants to leave Charlie a liferent of the farmhouse but a liferent provision in his will would be ineffective because he does not own the property to be liferented. A solution would be for the partnership to convey

> *the farmhouse to James so that he can create a liferent trust in his will leaving the liferent interest in the trust to Charlie and the capital interest to John and/or Jane. If Charlie had been a partner, the partnership agreement could be amended to allow Charlie liferent occupation of the farmhouse.*Discretionary Trusts

A discretionary trust can be set up in a will. The clause constituting the trust should identify a range of potential beneficiaries of the trust, by name or class, and the assets to be held in the trust. The executors of the will are the first trustees but more can be assumed as the trust progresses. It should be remembered that the trustees will have complete discretion over the management and disposal of the trust assets so their appointment should be carefully considered. The testator might also consider a letter of wishes to explain to the trustees why the discretionary trust has been set up and what the testator wants the trustees to do, without in any way encroaching on their unfettered discretion.

Discretionary trusts are subject to a ten yearly charge to inheritance tax at currently 6% of the value of the assets within the trust exceeding the nil rate band of £325,000. However, APR and BR apply to the value of the assets within the discretionary trust. If the whole trust assets are eligible for APR or BR, the charge to tax may be nil.

A discretionary trust may be useful when the farmer's children are relatively young and have not made final career decisions. The trustees could hold the farm in trust until a clear successor to the farming enterprise is identified. This may involve trustees being in office for many years and consideration should be given to whether the trustees should be entitled to remuneration for professional or indeed practical work.

Residue

The general rule is that any property belonging to the farmer which is not specifically bequeathed falls into the residue of their estate.

Care should be taken to make sure that the farmer understands exactly which assets are being specifically bequeathed and which fall into residue.

Alternate residuary beneficiaries should always be specified to avoid creating an intestacy where one or more of the residuary beneficiaries predeceases the farmer.

The exception to the general rule stated above is that the tenant's interest in an agricultural lease never falls into residue. It is either specifically bequeathed or it falls into intestacy.

CHAPTER SIX

EXECUTORS

When selecting executors any testator should be advised to choose individuals they trust to execute their wishes and at least one executor who is of a younger generation.

Clients should always be encouraged to discuss the appointment as executor with the chosen individual or individuals to ensure that they are content to accept the appointment.

Farming clients need to be especially careful when choosing executors. In addition to the above the farming client should consider the following points.

Practical Experience

A relatively young farmer making a will which would benefit minor children might want to consider appointing an executor with practical experience of farming to ensure that the farming business continues to run smoothly following a sudden death.

A farming relative or neighbour might be a good choice, perhaps acting alongside the deceased farmer's accountant or solicitor.

Where there is an expectation that the executor will have to devote a significant amount of time or actual work in the fulfilment of his or her duties, the testator might want to consider whether it would be appropriate for that person to be professionally remunerated for the work undertaken.

Unless the will specifically provides that the executor may receive such remuneration, he or she would be entitled only to their out of pocket expenses.

Conflict of Interest

A farmer making a will should be advised to consider whether their chosen executor will be able to act in good faith as executor or whether there could be a risk that the executor may have a conflict of interest.

For example:-

- If the executor is also a partner in the farming business and a dispute arose regarding the interpretation of the clause in the partnership agreement dealing with payment of a deceased partner's share, the executor may be conflicted.

- If the executor is involved in the farming business and is also one of several beneficiaries the executor may be conflicted, particularly in relation to any non-farming beneficiary, if the terms of the will provide for payment to non-farming beneficiaries from the farming business which is struggling financially to make those payments.

- If the executor is a co-tenant of a pro indiviso secure tenancy, the executor may be conflicted if required to choose a successor to the tenancy.

There is no way to know if a conflict of interest will arise in the future and if so, how the individual executor would act but it would be wise to consider appointing several executors representing the various interest groups for balance. The appointment of several executors allows those with no conflict of interest to make decisions where one executor is conflicted and excuses themself from taking decisions on the matter giving rise to the conflict of interest.

The testator could appoint one executor who is a practical farmer and a partner in the farming partnership, one executor who is not involved in the business, for example a non-farming child, and one professional executor such as a solicitor or accountant. In this instance three is most definitely not a crowd!

CHAPTER SEVEN

LEGAL RIGHTS

Legal Rights is the expression used to describe the statutory legal claims certain beneficiaries have on a deceased person's estate, regardless of the terms of the will.

In Scotland spouses, civil partners and children of the deceased are all entitled to claim Legal Rights. If Legal Rights are claimed the claimant must renounce any bequest in the will.

A spouse or civil partner can claim one third of the deceased's net moveable estate if the deceased has children, one half of the deceased's net moveable estate if the deceased had no children.

Children of the deceased can claim one third of the net moveable estate divided among them, thus if there are three children each child's claim is a one nineth share of the net moveable estate.

If there are children of the deceased but no spouse or civil partner then the children can claim one half of the net moveable estate divided among them, thus if there are three children each child's claim is a one sixth share of the net moveable estate.

The issue of a predeceasing child, who will be the grandchildren or remoter descendants of the deceased, can claim the Legal Rights to which their parent would have been entitled had he or she survived the deceased.

When preparing a will for a farmer the discussion around Legal Rights usually considers the potential for claims from non-farming children. It should be remembered however that spouses and civil partners have

Legal Rights claims too and that may be particularly relevant in step-family situations.

Legal rights are of particular concern to the farming community because farmers often have relatively large moveable estates.

The farmer's business structure will normally include moveable property, for example:-

- Shares in a private limited company.
- Assets of a sole trader business as shown on the balance sheet.
- Capital balance in a partnership

The latter may include the value of the farm itself if the farm is owned by the partnership or held in trust for the partnership and shown on the balance sheet. The farm becomes moveable because s22 of the Partnership Act 1890 applies (see Chapter 4).

The implications of Legal Rights should be fully explained to a farmer making a will.

If the farmer wishes to avoid a Legal Rights claim, the following options could be considered:-

1. **Reducing the extent of the moveable estate**

   This could be achieved by gifting assets as Potentially Exempt Transfers. An example would be gifting tranches of the farmer's capital balance in the partnership accounts to some or all of the other partners. Capital Gains Tax implications should always be considered. Other ideas might include removing the farm from the balance sheet, subject again to detailed tax advice, or setting up heritable capital accounts as noted above in Chapter 4.

2. Discharge of Legal Rights

If the farmer gifts assets to a child or spouse during their lifetime they may hope in doing so to avoid a later Legal Rights claim. The gift could be of heritable or moveable property. A useful Inheritance Tax planning measure would be to gift assets which will not qualify for Agricultural Property Relief or Business Relief as Potentially Exempt Transfers. In such a situation a discharge of Legal Rights might be sought from the donee. The discharge should be in writing and probative, ie signed and witnessed and preferably registered with the Books of Council and Session. A copy should be kept with the will. In order to avoid a future challenge, the deed should contain a declaration that the donee has taken independent legal advice or has been advised to do so and chosen not to. The Law Society of Scotland's guidance on having documents signed by third parties should also be followed.

CHAPTER EIGHT

TENANCIES

It is important to identity the type of tenancy the farmer enjoys so the solicitor drafting the will can deal with the tenancy appropriately.

The usual types of tenancy are:-

- 1991 Act tenancy
- Short Limited Duration Tenancy
- Modern Limited Duration Tenancy
- Limited Duration Tenancy
- Partnership Lease
- Grazing lease
- Repairing Lease

There are no statutory provisions regarding bequest of a Grazing Lease and such a contract falls on the death of the tenant unless otherwise provided in the lease itself.

Partnership Leases are a special type of 1991 Act tenancy where the Tenant is a partnership involving some combination of the Tenant and the Landlord or the Landlord's nominee.

Contract Farming Agreements are not leases and the contractor's interest in the agreement is not normally capable of assignation or bequest.

1991 Act Tenancies

Succession to 1991 Act tenancies is covered by s11 and s12 of the Agricultural Holdings (Scotland) Ace 1991 ("the 1991 Act"). These provisions apply to both leases in writing and unwritten leases.

s11 states a tenant may bequeath his interest in the tenancy to any person within a list of eligible legatees defined in s1A. This has to be done by a specific bequest –

> *"I bequeath the tenancy of Whiteknowes Farm to my son Hugh...".*

The list of potentially eligible legatees contains a wide range of relatives both by blood and marriage. Within this list of legatees is a privileged group known as the "near relatives" as defined in s10(A) (6) of the 1991 Act.

The bequest must be to one person only. If there is no specific bequest the lease does not fall into the residue of the estate, it falls into intestacy. The residuary beneficiary is not entitled to succeed to the lease where there is no specific legacy.

In terms of s11 (2) of the 1991 Act the legatee has to give notice to the Landlord within 21 days of the tenant's death. That is a very tight timescale within which to investigate whether there was a tenancy, whether the deceased bequeathed the tenancy in his or her will and then to take instructions from the legatee as to whether they wish to accept the bequest and if so to draft the notice and intimate it on the Landlord. The only exception to this time limit is where the legatee can show that he or she has been prevented from giving notice by "some unavoidable cause", ie severe illness. If the legatee does not accept the bequest the lease does not come to an end but the right to the lease is treated as intestate estate.

The Landlord has 30 days from receipt of the notice to object to the proposed legatee by serving a counter-notice intimating that the Landlord objects to receiving the legatee as the tenant under the lease. If the legatee is a "near relative" of the deceased the Landlord can only object under s12A(3) of the 1991 Act on the grounds that the legatee is not of good character, does not have sufficient resources to allow the legatee to farm the holding with reasonable efficiency or does not have sufficient training in agriculture or sufficient practical experience of farming to farm the holding with reasonable efficiency. This last ground of objection does not apply where the legatee is engaged in, or will begin within 6 months of the notice being given, a course of relevant training in agriculture which the person is expected satisfactorily to complete within 4 years from the date of the notice and in the meantime has arranged for the holding to be farmed with reasonable efficiency until the legatee completes that course.

If the Landlord serves a counter-notice he or she must follow up with a referral to the Land Court within one month of the date of the counter-notice. Where the Landlord fails to make such a referral to the Land Court the counter-notice ceases to have effect and the lease is binding on the legatee.

If the Landlord does make a referral to the Land Court and the court believes any ground of objection by the Landlord has been established then the Land Court must make an order declaring the bequest to be null and void.

If the legatee is not a "near relative" but one of the wider list of eligible legatees the Landlord can serve a counter-notice as above without giving any reason and within one month of the date of the counter-notice apply to the Land Court. Under s12B the onus of proof is reversed so the legatee must make the case and prove to the satisfaction of the Land Court that there is a "reasonable ground" for not declaring the bequest to be null and void. The near relative legatee is in a much stronger position.

Intestate Succession

Intestacy in agricultural law is not the same as intestacy under the general law. The rules on intestacy apply where there is no will, where there is a will but there is no specific bequest of the tenancy, where there was a specific bequest but the legatee rejected the bequest and where there was a specific bequest but it was declared null and void by the Land Court under s12A or s12B. These provisions are found in S16 of the Succession Scotland Act 1964. Where a legatee's intimation has been challenged by the Landlord and that challenge was successful the lease is not terminated. The executors have a second chance to deal with the tenancy under intestacy.

The executors confirm to the tenancy and then transfer it to an acquirer who then intimates to the Landlord. That whole process must be completed within one year of the date of death. During that period of one year from the date of death the executors can pay the rent as executors and this can safely be accepted by the Landlord without compromising the Landlord's ability to challenge the eventual acquirer. As with legacies, there can be only one acquirer.

The executor can nominate any person as an acquirer but the Landlord's consent is required where the acquirer is not a person entitled to succeed to the deceased's intestate estate or claim legal rights or prior rights on the deceased's estate.

The acquirer must intimate to the Landlord that he or she has acquired the tenancy within 21 days of the acquisition. The Landlord has the same opportunity to object to a near relative acquirer under s12A and any other acquirer under s12B and the same provisions for referral to the Land Court apply.

A Tenant making a will must consider very carefully whether or not to make a specific bequest of the tenancy. A bequest might be prohibited by the lease or the legatee might fail to take the necessary action within 21 days of the Tenant's death. It may be preferable to allow the tenancy to fall into intestacy because the time limit of one year from date of death to transfer the tenancy to an acquirer is much longer. If a Tenant would rather allow the tenancy to fall into intestacy but wants to give his or her executors some direction an expression of wish could be drafted as part of the will or as a separate testamentary writing. It must be made clear that the expression of wish is not a bequest, eg

> *"Without making any specific bequest of my tenancy of Whiteknowes Farm I express the wish that my executors consider transferring the said tenancy to my son Hugh".*

Joint Tenants

It is not unusual for leases to be granted to more than one tenant or for other tenants to be added to leases. If that is the case then the interest of the deceased person might pass on survivorship or the tenancy might be held by two or more tenants in pro indiviso shares. If the lease was in favour of X and Y and the survivor and X dies then Y becomes the sole tenant but if the lease was in favour of X and Y with no survivorship destination then when X dies his executors have to deal with a pro indiviso interest in the tenancy so all of the above applies but instead of referring to the tenancy as a whole the reference is to a pro indiviso share.

SLDTs, LDTs, MLDTs and Repairing Leases

The modern forms of agricultural tenancy are also capable of being transferred on the death of the original tenant. As these tenancies have a fixed duration their value to a legatee or acquirer is less than a 1991 Act tenancy. The procedure the executors should follow is similar to the above and is set out in sections s20, s21 and s22 of the 2003 Act.

S21 of the 2003 Act provides that a Tenant may bequeath the tenancy and applies the same definition of eligible legatees and near relatives as apply to 1991 Act tenancies. The legatee must give notice to the Landlord of the bequest within 21 days of the death of the Tenant. The Landlord can serve a counter-notice objecting to the Tenant within one month of receiving the notice. The grounds of objection are the same in relation to near relatives and other persons as those for 1991 Act tenancies.

S16 of the 1964 Act is specifically applied to SLDTs, LDTs, MLDTs and Repairing Tenancies by s20 of the 2003 Act. The executors of the deceased tenant can transfer the tenancy on "intestacy", ie where there is legal intestacy, where there is no specific bequest of the tenancy, where the legatee rejects the bequest or where the bequest is declared null and void. The executors transfer the tenancy to the person they have selected and that person must give notice to the Landlord within 21 days of the transfer.

The Landlord can object to the transfer and apply to the Land Court on the same grounds as he or she could have objected to the transfer of a 1991 Act tenancy. However, in relation to 2003 Act tenancies the Landlord has another potential course of action. The executors can transfer the tenancy to any person but where that person is not a person who would have been entitled to inherit the deceased's estate on intestacy or claim legal rights or prior rights in relation to that estate then the Landlord can give notice under s22(3) within 30 days of receiving the notice of transfer that he or she intends to acquire the tenant's interest in the lease.

The 2003 Act imposes a limit on the discretion of the executors to choose a potential successor to the lease on intestacy. Any transfer of the lease must be in "the best interests of the deceased's estate."

Partnership Leases

Succession to these tenancies depends on the terms of the partnership agreement. Some end on the death of the general partner and some allow for assignation of the general partner's interest. S72 of the 2003 Act provides that if the Landlord tries to terminate the lease by terminating the partnership (meaning the Tenant no longer exists) then the general partner can become a secure Tenant as an individual if the notice procedure is followed. That section does not apply if the partnership ends because the Tenant dies, only if the Landlord does something to terminate the partnership. If the partnership agreement terminates on the death of the general partner then s72 will not save the tenancy.

CHAPTER NINE

PARTNERSHIPS

This chapter will summarise the relevance of Partnership Agreements when making wills and consider how a bequest of a partnership share is made. If the Partnership Agreement predates the will and its terms conflict with the will then the Partnership Agreement will be given precedence.

Partnership Agreements

Other sections of this book have dealt with various aspects of partnership agreements which are relevant to wills.

These are:-

- Ensuring the partnership agreement has a relevant continuation clause so it does not terminate on the death of one partner.

- Checking whether a statement has been made in the agreement itself, a subsequent amendment or a partnership minute that s22 of the Partnership (Scotland) Act 1890 has been disapplied to the effect that heritable property does not become moveable by virtue of that statutory provision but remains heritable.

- Checking the provisions on repayment of capital and establishing whether book value or market value of assets is to be used in accounts to date of death.

Legacy of Partnership Share

A typical legacy of a partnership share would be:-

> *I direct my executors to make over to my daughter Arabella my whole interest of whatever kind in the firm of ABC Farmers, a partnership formed under the law of Scotland and having a place of business at Darklands Farm, Caldwell, in the County of Perth as it is presently constituted or as it may be constituted at the time of my death.*

Although it is obvious to legal professionals, it is sometimes not clear to clients that the object of the legacy is the capital balance within the partnership accounts. There is often a misconception that the beneficiary becomes a partner in place of the deceased. That is not the case, a new partner cannot be imposed unilaterally on the continuing partners by the deceased.

Sometimes the beneficiary is already a partner. In that situation the partnership accountant will simply transfer the deceased's share to the beneficiary partner in the accounts so the beneficiary's own capital balance will increase in amount equivalent to the deceased's capital balance.

If the beneficiary is not already a partner the legacy of the capital balance is effectively a debt due by the partnership to the deceased's estate. The Partnership Agreement may provide that the sums due are paid over a period of five or ten years. The intention is that the repayments could be made from trading income but if the capital balance is high and trading conditions in farming are not good that may not be possible. It is important that the testator understands the extent of the burden of paying out their capital share.

Most partnership agreements provide that interest is paid on the outstanding capital balance until payment. Remember that the interest may be substantial especially if the capital balance includes the value of some or all of the farm. Where the capital balance is £2.5 million the relatively benign interest rate of 1% above base lending rate results in an annual interest payment of £43,750. Often older Partnership Agreements will show interest rates of 4% or 5% above base lending rate.

This is an example showing the difference in value between a legacy of a partnership share including the farm and a legacy of the farm itself.

> *Scenario 1*
>
> *David is a partner in Daveco Farming. The partnership owns Sunnyside Farm which is the sole asset of the partnership. David dies. His will bequeaths his share of the partnership to his girlfriend Susie. The partnership agreement provides for revaluation of assets on death. Sunnyside Farm is valued at £1,500,000 at the date of David's death. David is one of three partners and the proportionate share of the value due to his estate is £500,000. That amount is paid out to Susie by the continuing partners at £100,000 per year for five years as provided for in the partnership agreement.*
>
> *Scenario 2*
>
> *David owns a one third share of Sunnyside Farm. David dies. His will bequeaths his share of the farm to his girlfriend Susie. The farm is valued at £1,500,000 at the date of David's death. The owners of the remaining two thirds of the farm try to negotiate with Susie to buy her inherited share of the farm for £500,000. Negotiations break down. Susie insists the farm is sold and threatens to raise an action of division and sale. On the open market the sale price is £3,000,000. Susie's share is £1,000,000.*

The difference in the amount due to Susie in the two scenarios is striking. The point to note is that a legacy of a partnership share means a legacy of an asset with an accounting value fixed at date of death whereas a legacy of the asset itself my increase (or exceptionally decrease) after the date of death.

CHAPTER TEN

OTHER FARMING ASSETS

This chapter lists various other farming assets often encountered when making a will for a farmer.

Tenants Improvements

If the farmer is a tenant farmer, and particularly if he or she is the tenant of a 1991 Act tenancy, there may be an accumulated value in tenant's improvements.

Tenants improvements fall into different categories with different procedures for intimation to the Landlord, see Schedule 5 of the Agricultural Holdings (Scotland) Act 1991.

A list of tenants improvements may have been agreed between the Landlord and the Tenant or may have been the subject of Land Court proceedings under the "Tenant's Amnesty" provisions introduced by the Land Reform (Scotland) Act 2016. Such a list is a useful and reasonably up to date record of improvements carried out by the tenant.

The person succeeding to the tenancy will inherit the value of these improvements.

Basic Payment Scheme Entitlements

Basic Payment Scheme Entitlements are used to claim financial support from the Scottish Government. The entitlements usually belong to the trading entity, eg a partnership of limited company.

If the farmer trades as a sole trader they will belong to the farmer in their individual name. A legacy of a sole trader business should therefore make specific reference to the entitlements.

Pedigree Stock and Hefted flocks

If the farmer owns a pedigree cattle herd or a pedigree sheep flock those individual animals will be worth more than average cattle or sheep. In addition, there is value in the herd or flock, the blood line of which may have been refined over many generations of the farmer's family.

Hill ground in Scotland is largely unfenced. Sheep grazing on hills could travel miles from the farm while grazing. A hefted flock is a flock of sheep of mixed ages where the older sheep know the area of the hill where they should graze and, in theory, they do not stray onto other properties.

A hefted flock has a value to the farmer and any successor whether as owner or tenant of the farm.

CHAPTER ELEVEN

INHERITANCE TAX RELIEFS

Farmers are usually able to claim either or both Agricultural Property Relief (APR) and Business Relief (BR) from Inheritance Tax on their assets.

When making a will for a farmer, it is important to establish which of their assets will qualify for these reliefs and identify any that will not qualify for either relief.

Any assets identified as not qualifying for APR or BR could be liable to inheritance tax. At the point of drafting the will, consideration could be given to lifetime gifting or bequeathing these assets to a spouse or civil partner as an exempt recipient.

Most farmers will use the services of an accountant and this kind of detailed succession planning is best carried out with advice from that accountant to avoid any potential Capital Gains Tax or Inheritance Tax pitfalls.

Agricultural Property Relief

The Inheritance Tax Act 1984 defines agricultural property as:-

> *agricultural land or pasture and includes woodland and any building used in connection with the intensive rearing of livestock or fish if the woodland or building is occupied with agricultural land or pasture and the occupation is ancillary to that of the agricultural land or pasture; and also includes such*

> *cottages, farm buildings and farmhouses, together with the land occupied with them, as are of a character appropriate to the property*

Any such property potentially qualifies for 100% APR. Only the agricultural value of the property is exempt. The agricultural value is the value which would be the value of the property if it were subject to a "perpetual covenant" prohibiting its use otherwise than as agricultural property.

A field next to the local village might have an agricultural value of £10,000. If outline planning consent has been obtained for residential development of the field the market value might be £1,000,000. APR is only available on the agricultural value of £10,000.

The agricultural property must be located within the UK but can be owned or let. The relief only applies where the agricultural property has been owned by the deceased for two years prior to date of death if the property is owned or for seven years prior to the date of death if occupied by someone else.

Assets commonly owned by farmers which do not benefit from APR but might benefit from BR include mast sites, quarries and diversified businesses such as farm shops or cafes.

Assets commonly owned by farmers which generally do not benefit from either APR or BR include:- farm cottages not occupied by farm workers, grandiose farm houses out of keeping with the character of the farm and holiday lets. This is a complex area of tax law beyond the scope of this book. Recent cases suggest that some let properties may qualify for BR if they are a relatively small part of the overall working farm. Specialist tax advice should be sought regarding these types of assets.

APR is claimed as part of the process of submitting a deceased person's estate to HMRC. The current form used to claim APR is form IHT414. It is useful to consider some of the questions posed on that form when discussing with a farmer whether or not property will qualify for agricultural property relief.

The questions include:-

- When and how did the deceased acquire the holding?
- Was the holding or any part of it subject to a binding contract for sale at the date of death?
- Are there any outstanding planning consents on the holding which have not been implemented?
- Give a detailed description of the day-to-day farming activities carried out on the land throughout the seven years prior to the date of death
- Give details of the extent of the deceased's involvement in those activities
- Give a full description of any farm buildings from which agricultural relief is deducted stating who was using them and for what purpose.

Buisness Relief

S 105 of the Inheritance Tax Act 1984 defines "relevant business property" as

(a) Property consisting of a business or interest in a business

(b) Securities of a company which are unquoted and which gave the deceased control of the company immediately before death

(c) Any unquoted shares in a company

(d) Shares or securities in a company which are quoted and which gave the deceased control of the company immediately before death

(e) Any land or building, machinery or plant, which, immediately before death was used wholly or mainly for the purposes of a business carried on by a company of which the deceased then had control or by a partnership of which he was then a partner and

(f) Any land or building, machinery or plant which, immediately before death was used wholly or mainly for the purposes of a business carried on by the deceased and was settled property in which he was then beneficially entitled to an interest in possession

Business Relief, previously known as Business Property Relief, is often seen as subsidiary to APR but in fact many farming estates are covered entirely by BR not APR. A farmer's capital balance in a partnership is treated as Business Property not agricultural property.

"Business" means a business carried on for gain. Business property can qualify for relief from inheritance tax at two rates, 50% or 100%.

Business Property falling within categories (a), (b) and (c) above qualifies for relief at 100%. Business Property falling within categories (d), (e) and (f) qualifies for relief at 50%.

The Business Property must have been owned by the deceased for at least two years prior to the date of death.

Business Relief does not apply where the nature of the business is making or holding investments. As noted above, a farm cottage which is let out to someone other than an agricultural worker is treated as an investment asset and only eligible for business relief in some restricted circumstances where the investment element forms only a small part of the overall farm business.

The current HMRC form used to claim BR is IHT 413. It is useful to consider some of the questions posed on that form when discussing with a farmer whether or not property will qualify for BR.

The questions include:-

- Did the deceased own the business interest throughout the two years prior to date of death?

- Was the whole or any part of the business, interest in a business, or were any of the business assets, subject to a binding contract for sale at the date of death?

- Is the business a partnership? If so, who provided the capital, what contribution did each person make to the capital and how are the profits shared?

Property does not qualify for BR if it would also qualify for APR so APR should be claimed first.

Whereas the Inheritance Act 1984 refers to "transferor" and " transfer", I have referred to "deceased" and "death" for clarity as we are dealing in this chapter with transfer under a will following death.

Residence Nil Rate Band

Residence Nil Rate Band (RNRB) can be claimed where the deceased's estate includes a residence which is inherited by descendants of the deceased.

There are complex provisions on tapering but generally speaking the RNRB cannot be claimed where value of the estate exceeds £2,000,000.00.

The current rate of RNRB is £175,000 which has been frozen until April 2026. Each person has their own RNRB which is transferable between spouses and civil partners. If a residence is left to a spouse or civil partner but passes to one or more direct descendants of the couple on the second death, the estate of the second person to die can claim RNRB and Transferable RNRB.

Most farmhouses qualify for APR. It is worth remembering RNRB may also be available if the deceased ever lived in any of the other houses on the farm.

For example:-

> *Bill lives in the farmhouse of the farm he owns. When he was younger he lived in one of the farm cottages. His great aunt Euphemia now lives in the cottage. On Bill's death, he bequeaths the farm including the farmhouse and the cottage to his daughter Sally. The cottage where Euphemia lives would not qualify for APR but may qualify for RNRB, depending on the extent of Bill's estate.*

RNRB may also assist where the farmhouse is not of a character appropriate to the farm and does not qualify for APR.

RNRB, rather unfairly, only applies to bequests to direct descendants. In the above example, if Euphemia owned the cottage and bequeathed it to Sally, RNRB could not be claimed on Euphemia's death.

CHAPTER TWELVE

PROVIDING FOR THE NON-FARMING CHILD

As with most testators, farming clients generally want to provide for their families in a way that is fair to all concerned.

Farming clients tend to have a specific problem in that the value of the farm usually far outweighs any other non-farming assets which could be bequeathed to family members who are not involved in the farming enterprise.

All families are different. A farming client might tell you that one child has worked hard on the farm since leaving school for very little financial return and another child has benefited from a university education funded by the farming business. In that case a fair division of assets might not be an equal division.

Once the farmer has decided what proportion of assets it would be reasonable for the non-farming child to receive consideration has to be given to the subject matter of that bequest.

Examples of ways in which the non-farming child can be provided for include:-

Non-core assets

If the farming business owns assets the removal of which would not affect the long-term running of the farming operation consideration should be given to bequeathing these assets to the non-farming child. Non-core assets include areas of woodland, cottages not used for farm workers, holiday cabins, quarries, turbines, farm shops, telecoms masts and land with development potential.

Some of these assets do not attract either APR or BR so if they are to be bequeathed to the non-farming child consideration should be given to making these over in lifetime as Potentially Exempt Transfers (PETS). A discharge of Legal Rights might be required if the lifetime gift is of substantial value.

Life Insurance

Depending on the age and risk profile of the testator, life insurance can be a relatively cheap and easy way to provide a cash sum for the non-farming child.

Security over the Farm

If the farm is being left to one child the testator might be concerned that the beneficiary would sell the farm. Whilst any non-farming children might be reasonably content to accept that their sibling has inherited the farm to keep the family business running, they would be somewhat disaffected if that sibling sells the farm at a vast profit.

One solution to that concern would be for the bequest of the farm to be subject to a security in favour of the non-farming children to give them a right to share in the sale proceeds if the farm is sold within a certain period after the testator's death. This effectively operates as a "claw-back" security with the will forming the underlying agreement constituting the debt.

The same procedure could be used to ensure a pay out of a cash legacy funded by the farming business over a number of years.

Example

Morna and Peter farm in partnership with their son Gavin. The farm is owned by Morna and occupied by the farming partnership. As well as the traditional farming business the couple run a successful farm shop and holiday letting business. There is a telecoms mast on the farm and the partnership has recently entered into an option agreement with a solar farm developer. Peter's capital balance in the partnership accounts is £600,000 and Morna's capital balance in the partnership accounts is £15,000. Morna and Peter have two other children together – Josie is a vet and lives in one of the farm cottages and Ian is an accountant who lives in Edinburgh. Peter has a daughter, Alice, from a previous relationship. The couple want to ensure that Gavin can continue to farm but they want to be fair to Josie and Ian. They are not in contact with Alice and Peter does not want to include her in his will.

Key points:-

- *The farm is owned by Morna but Peter has a high capital balance in the partnership. Peter could transfer some or all of that capital to Morna and/or Gavin to reduce any potential legal rights claim by Alice.*

- *Morna intends to leave the farm to Gavin. She might want to put in place provisions whereby if the farm was sold within ten years of her death some of the sale price would be shared with Ian and Josie.*

- *The farming business could continue although some non-core assets were bequeathed or gifted in lifetime to Josie and Ian. For example, Morna could gift the farm cottage where Josie lives to her. This asset will probably not qualify for inheritance tax relief and could be gifted to Josie as a potentially exempt transfer. If the farming partnership does not require the income, consideration could be given to gifting the mast site and solar panel site to Josie and Ian to equalise their inheritance with Gavin.*

- *The farm shop may qualify for BR. The holiday letting business may or may not qualify for BR. These assets could be gifted to Josie and Ian in lifetime or by bequest.*

- *Lifetime gifting should be recorded for IHT purposes.*

- *Morna and Peter's wills could narrate lifetime gifting which has taken place as a record of fairness amongst the family and Legal Rights discharges may be sought from Josie and Ian in exchange for lifetime gifts.*

CHAPTER THIRTEEN

OTHER CONSIDERATIONS

This final chapter deals with a few matters distinct from but related to will drafting for farmers.

Future Review of Will

The making of a will is a hugely significant event for some farmers and there is a tendency to attempt to cover all future possible scenarios in the will and once completed to consider it to be set in stone.

Whilst no-one wants the expense of changing a will on a regular basis, farmers should be encouraged to make their wills based on the current situation with a suggestion that they review the will at a specific future date, five or ten years in the future, or when a particular event happens, for example when a child decides their future career.

Keeping a will under regular review can be preferable to creating an overly complex document which attempts to foretell the future.

Wills for Other Family Members

The solicitor should ask if wills for any other family members are required. Not only is this good business but it can ensure that careful succession planning in one generation does not go awry in the next. If a famer bequeaths their farming assets to one child and that child dies intestate the farmer's wishes may not end up being carried out. The solicitor should of course be mindful of rules on conflict of interest and the farmer should be advised that their family members can changer their wills at any time.

Power of Attorney

If the farmer does not already have a power of attorney in place, the meeting to discuss their will is a good opportunity to suggest a power of attorney should also be prepared.

In addition to the usual points a solicitor would discuss with a client making a power of attorney, the following should be considered:-

1. Does the chosen attorney have the requisite practical experience to run the business or direct the running of the business if required?

2. What powers will the attorney specifically need to run the business and how should these be drafted in the deed?

3. Should the attorney also have power on behalf of the granter to resign as a director or partner so that the now incapax farmer can exit the business structure?

4. What powers to gift will the attorney need to implement or progress a succession plan?

All of the above should be discussed in detail with the farmer so their views can be given effect to in the deed.

Care Home Costs

As with any high net worth individual, farmers need to consider how they will fund their care in the future.

If the farmer required long term residential care their assets including the capital in the farming partnership, the value of the sole trader business, the private company shares or even the farm itself, would be assessed by the Local Authority as part of the process of means testing the farmer's liability to contribute to the cost of their care.

The farmer should consider whether such care home costs could easily be met from trading income and if not, identify assets which could be sold to meet the costs.

Early succession planning could ensure that assets have already been safely transferred to the next generation but it is worth bearing in mind that the Local Authority can challenge such gifting if they consider the farmer has intentionally deprived themselves of assets to avoid liability for care home costs.

Deeds of Variation

At the present time executors and beneficiaries have the opportunity to rewrite a deceased person's will using a Deed of Variation. A Deed of Variation is often used to make the original will more tax efficient.

Deeds of variation must be completed within two years of the deceased person's death. More than one deed of variation can be entered into provided all of the deeds are signed within two years of date of death. However, where an asset has been dealt with in a deed of variation, a subsequent deed of variation cannot deal again with the same asset.

The current government guidance on Deeds of Variation (form IOV2) states:-

> *For a variation to take effect for IHT and/or CGT purposes, it must contain a statement that those signing the variation intend it to take effect for tax purposes. The statement may*

> *apply to either IHT or CGT alone or for both taxes. The statement must include the appropriate statutory references. For example, a statement such as "The parties to this variation intend that the provisions of section 142(1) Inheritance Tax Act 1984 and section 62(6) Taxation of Chargeable Gains Act 1992 shall apply" would mean that the variation is to take effect for both IHT and CGT.*

Farmers should not rely on the current rules about Deeds of Variation when making their wills. The rules may change in the future and Deeds of Variation may no longer be allowed. Those whose entitlements are being varied must all be in agreement to change the terms of the will so one dissenting party could prevent a Deed of Variation being entered into.

CHAPTER FOUTEEN

A WORKED EXAMPLE

Morag is a farmer. She owns Farside Farm in her own name. She is the tenant of a 1991 Act tenancy of Nearside Farm and a Short Limited Duration Tenancy of the local Church of Scotland Glebe.

Morag farms in partnership with her life partner Fred and daughter Katie. The partnership trades as Farside Farmers and owns two fields known as the Low Fields adjacent to the nearest village. The couple also have a son, Oliver, who is a social media influencer. No-one understands what he actually does but it is very lucrative and he uses the farm setting as a backdrop for his videos.

Both Katie and Oliver live in cottages on the farm.

Another cottage on the farm has been renovated and is now used for holiday letting.

Morag and Fred sell honey produced on the farm directly to the public from a roadside farm shop. They incorporated a company, Farside Honey Ltd to operate the business. Morag owns 100% of the shares in the company.

Under close questioning Morag reveals that she is still married to Derek with whom she had a daughter, Claire. Following her separation from Derek, he and Claire moved to Australia.

Key points to identify

- Farside Farm is owned by Morag as an individual

- There is a 1991 Act Tenancy of Nearside Farm
- There is a Short Limited Duration Tenancy of the Glebe Land
- Morag has a capital balance in the partnership which includes ownership of the Low Fields
- The Low Fields might have development potential
- There is a separate company which owns and operates the honey business
- The holiday letting cottage is owned by Morag but the business is operated as part of the partnership farming business.

Morag's objectives are:-

- To see the farming business continued by the next generation, probably by Katie
- To provide security for Fred and Oliver in addition to the provision made for Katie
- To avoid inheritance tax
- To ensure that neither Derek nor Claire has any claim on her estate

There are a number of different ways to achieve Morag's objectives. There is more than one possible solution but the draft will in Appendix 1 leaves the farming assets to Katie, the cottage where he lives to Oliver and a liferent interest in the farmhouse to Fred.

Morag's will is however only part of the solution.

In order to minimise inheritance tax Morag might wish to consider:-

- Conveying the cottage where he lives to Oliver now as Potentially Exempt Transfer. The cottage is unlikely to qualify for Agricultural Relief as it is not occupied by a farm worker.

- The holiday letting cottage may or may not qualify for Business Relief as part of the overall partnership assets. It could be conveyed now to Oliver, Fred or Katie as a potentially exempt transfer provided the income is not required to subsidise the farming income of the partnership.

- The Low Fields will only qualify for Agricultural Relief to the extent of their agricultural value. Any hope value or development value will be subject to inheritance tax. Again, a potentially exempt transfer might be considered with a discharge of Legal Rights if appropriate.

Detailed Capital Gains Tax advice would be required.

In order to minimise any claim by Derek and Claire, Morag might wish to consider:-

- Divorcing Derek to defeat his legal rights claim

- Reducing her moveable estate by transferring some or all of the shares in Farside Honey Ltd to Fred and some or all of the partnership capital to Fred or Katie.

Of course, if Morag did divorce Derek she could marry Fred and any lifetime gift to him would be free of capital gains tax and any bequest free of inheritance tax.

APPENDIX ONE

STYLE WILL BASED ON CHAPTER 14 EXAMPLE

I, MORAG FARMER, residing at Farside Farm, Ingleside, Perth in order to settle the succession to my estate after my death provide as follows:-

1. REVOCATION

   I revoke all prior wills and testamentary writings.

2. EXECUTORS

   I appoint my partner Fred Smith, residing with me at Farside Farm aforesaid, my daughter KATIE FARMER and my son OLIVER FARMER, both also residing at Farside Farm aforesaid to be my executors.

3. INFORMAL WRITINGS

   I direct my executors to give effect to all (if any) informal writings dated after the date hereof and written in my own hand or subscribed or initialled by me, however otherwise informal the same may be, if my executors are satisfied as to the authenticity of the same, declaring that my executors shall be the sole judges as to the validity, meaning and effect of any such writing; And the decision of my executors thereon shall be final and binding on all beneficiaries hereunder and under any codicil hereto.

4. LEGACIES

Unless otherwise specified any legacy granted by any writing shall be paid or made over as soon as my executors consider practicable after my death, free of taxes in respect of my death and of expenses, but without interest.

5. LEGACIES OF FURNITURE AND EFFECTS

I direct my executors to make over to the said Fred Smith, as an individual all my articles of personal, domestic, household, garage or leisure use, ornament or consumption and my motor vehicles and that in such way as they may agree or failing such agreement as my executors in their sole discretion shall consider approximately equal and fair.

6. LEGACY OF COTTAGE

I direct my executors to make over to the said Oliver Farmer, as an individual, the heritable property known as Cottage No. 2, Farside Farm, aforesaid free of all expenses of transfer, heritable debts and securities, and other capital burdens affecting the farm at the time of my death.

7. LEGACY OF IN HAND FARM

Under exception of Cottage No. 2 bequethed in Clause 7 hereof, and subject to the provisions of Clause 10 hereof, I direct my executors to make over to the said Katie Farmer, as an individual, the farm and lands of Farside Farm including the farm buildings, free of all expenses of transfer, heritable debts and securities, and other capital burdens affecting the farm at the time of my death.

8. LEGACY OF FARM TENANCY

I direct my executors to make over to my said daughter Katie Farmer, as an individual:-

8.1. my interest in the tenancy of the farm and lands of Nearside, free of all expenses of transfer, heritable debts and securities, and any other capital burdens affecting my interest at the time of my death, together with the whole stock and the value of any tenants improvements so far as belonging to me at the time of my death;

8.2. my interest in the tenancy of the Ingleside Glebe free of all expenses of transfer, heritable debts and securities, and any other capital burdens affecting my interest at the time of my death, together with the whole stock and the value of any tenants improvements so far as belonging to me at the time of my death

9. LIFERENT TO FRED SMITH

I direct my trustees to retain the farmhouse at Farside Farm aforesaid (hereinafter referred to as "the Farmhouse") in a liferent trust for the said Fred Smith as an individual. The said Fred Smith shall be responsible for maintaining the Farmhouse in at least as good condition as it is at the date of my death; for paying all outgoings of whatever nature in relation to the Farmhouse including without prejudice to that generality all maintenance, insurance, Council Tax or any tax levied in substitute therefor, telephone and utility bills and all others. The foregoing liferent will terminate on the death of the said Fred Smith, should he renounce the said liferent or should he go into long term care to the reasonable satisfaction of my Trustees. On termination of the said liferent I direct my executors to make over the Farmhouse to my said daughter, Katie Farmer as an individual. Declaring that should the said Katie Farmer predecease the date of vesting leaving issue (including adopted issue) who shall survive the date of vesting each member of a generation of issue of such predeceasing child shall share equally in the part of my estate both original and accresced which would have fallen to its parent if in life. Vesting shall occur on the date or dates of failure, renunciation or termination of the foregoing liferent.

10. LEGACY OF PRIVATE COMPANY SHARES

I direct my executors to make over to the said Fred Smith, as an individual all my shares and stock of whatever classes in Farside Honey Limited (Company number SC12345) or such other shares or stock as may represent the same at the time of my death as a result of any amalgamation takeover or reorganisation of this company as to which my executors shall be the sole judges.

11. LEGACY OF PARTNERSHIP INTEREST

I direct my executors to make over to the said Katie Farmer, as an individual my whole interest of whatever kind in the firm of Farside Farmers as it is presently constituted or as it may be constituted at the time of my death.

12. RESIDUE

I direct my executors to make over the residue of my estate to the said Fred Smith as an individual; declaring that should the said Fred Smith pre-decease me I direct my executors to make over the residue of my estate to such of my children the said Katie Farmer and Oliver Farmer who shall survive me equally between them and the survivor of them; Declaring that should either of the said Katie Farmer or Oliver Farmer predecease leaving issue (including adopted issue) who shall survive me each member of a generation of issue of such predeceasing child shall share equally in the part of my estate both original and accresced which would have fallen to its parent if in life.

13. POWERS

13.1. My executors shall have the fullest powers of retention, realisation, investment, appropriation, transfer of property without realisation, and management of my estate as if they were absolute owners and not executors.

13.2. My executors may resign office notwithstanding any benefit under this will.

13.3. My executors may appoint one or more of their own number to act as solicitor or agent in any other capacity and allow that executor the same remuneration to which that executor would have been entitled if not an executor.

14. DOMICILE

I declare that my domicile is Scottish.

15. FUNERAL INSTRUCTIONS

I wish my body to be buried in the High Field at Farside Farm aforesaid.

TESTING CLAUSE

This document is executed as follows:-

It is subscribed by me the said Morag Farmer at the place and on the date undernoted in the presence of the witness hereunto subscribing:-

APPENDIX TWO

STYLE DISCHARGE OF LEGAL RIGHTS

I, ** *name and designation of potential claimant* ** CONSIDERING that in terms of the Succession (Scotland) Act 1964 I have entitlement to a ***fraction representing potential claimant's entitlement*** share of the legitim fund in the estate of my ** *relationship to the testator followed by full name and designation of testator*** ("my entitlement") and have been advised of the estimated amount of my entitlement; FURTHER CONSIDERING that my ***relationship to testator* ** has made a lifetime gift to me of ** *describe property or sum of money gifted* **; FURTHER CONSIDERING that I have been advised to take separate and independent legal advice in respect of my said entitlements and have done so and following the taking of said separate and independent legal advice have agreed to grant these presents; THEREFORE I do hereby DISCHARGE now and in all time coming my entitlement to claim legal rights from the net moveable estate of my said ** *relationship to testator* ** and I Do Hereby EXONER and DISCHARGE my ***relationship to testator*** executors in that respect; And I confirm that these presents are freely granted by me and are irrevocable: IN WITNESS WHEREOF

APPENDIX THREE

STYLE PARTNERSHIP AGREEMENT CLAUSE – HERITABLE PROPERTY

It is specifically agreed that the farm and lands of ***describe farm*** (hereinafter referred to as "the farm") and any other land or heritable property of the Partnership shall be treated as heritable and not moveable for the purposes of Section 22 of the Partnership Act 1890 between the Partners (including the representatives of a deceased Partner), and also as between heirs and successors of a deceased Partner and his executors.

The Partners agree that the capital accounts of each of the Partners shall be organised so that they will show separate Heritable Capital Accounts for each Partner which Heritable Capital Accounts will together equal the value of the Farm. Each of the Partners ***or specify which partner or partners*** shall be entitled to a proportionate share of the profits (and shall bear all of the losses) of a capital nature in relation to the Farm.

APPENDIX FOUR

CHECKLIST –
WILL FOR FARMER

Client Personal Details

- Name
- Address
- Contact Number and Email
- Date of Birth
- AML documentation up to date?

Client Family Details

- Name of Spouse/Civil Partner
- Children's full names and dates of birth

Family Tree

Consider potential Legal Rights Claims

Initial Advice

- Does the client have capacity?
- Are there any previous wills to be located and destroyed?

Extent of the Estate

- Who owns the farm?
- How does the business trade? Eg sole trader/partnership/private limited company
- Check business accounts, title deeds, partnership agreement.

Testamentary Wishes

- Appointment of executors – consider if practical experience will be required and whether there are any potential conflicts of interest.
- Legacies
- Residuary beneficiaries
- Consider whether any liferent or discretionary trusts required to hold assets for incapax beneficiaries or for asset protection

Inheritance Tax

- Testator's assets
- Previous Potentially Exempt Transfers
- Availability of transferable nil rate band, residence nil rate band and transferable residence nil rate band
- Identify assets which should benefit from Agricultural Relief or Business Relief

Guardians

Funeral Instructions

Any other matters

- Power of attorney required?
- Detailed IHT advice required?
- Residential care costs planning advice required?
- Should any other family members make wills?

APPENDIX FIVE

STYLE CLAUSES FOR POWER OF ATTORNEY

1. Power to make gifts

To make gifts to any family member whether or not I may previously have made gifts to that person and whether out of excess income or out of capital and even although by making such gifts I acknowledge that my Attorney may diminish my estate, provided, however, that my Attorney shall not make such gifts if by so doing my estate is diminished to such an extent that my estate, taking into account all income which I might receive including payments of pensions, dividend income, payments from the State in respect of Care or Attendance Allowances or others, would not be sufficient to keep me in relative comfort for the remainder of my life in respect of which my Attorney shall be the sole judge.

2. Power to resign

On my behalf to intimate my resignation *from the firm of* ****/as a director of* *** and to serve the requisite notice or notices to give effect to that resignation and to complete all other documentation required to facilitate that resignation and to call on *the firm of* ****/company of* *** fully to account for all sums due to me from the said *firm of/company of* and to receive on my behalf all such sums due to me.

'A Practical Guide to the EU Succession Regulation' by Richard Frimston
'A Practical Guide to Solicitor and Client Costs – 2nd Edition' by Robin Dunne
'Constructive Dismissal – Practice Pointers and Principles' by Benjimin Burgher
'A Practical Guide to Religion and Belief Discrimination Claims in the Workplace' by Kashif Ali
'A Practical Guide to the Law of Medical Treatment Decisions' by Ben Troke
'Fundamental Dishonesty and QOCS in Personal Injury Proceedings: Law and Practice' by Jake Rowley
'A Practical Guide to the Law in Relation to School Exclusions' by Charlotte Hadfield & Alice de Coverley
'A Practical Guide to Divorce for the Silver Separators' by Karin Walker
'The Right to be Forgotten – The Law and Practical Issues' by Melissa Stock
'A Practical Guide to Planning Law and Rights of Way in National Parks, the Broads and AONBs' by James Maurici QC, James Neill et al
'A Practical Guide to Election Law' by Tom Tabori
'A Practical Guide to the Law in Relation to Surrogacy' by Andrew Powell
'A Practical Guide to Claims Arising from Fatal Accidents – 2nd Edition' by James Patience
'A Practical Guide to the Ownership of Employee Inventions – From Entitlement to Compensation' by James Tumbridge & Ashley Roughton
'A Practical Guide to Asbestos Claims' by Jonathan Owen & Gareth McAloon
'A Practical Guide to Stamp Duty Land Tax in England and Northern Ireland' by Suzanne O'Hara
'A Practical Guide to the Law of Farming Partnerships' by Philip Whitcomb
'Covid-19, Homeworking and the Law – The Essential Guide to Employment and GDPR Issues' by Forbes Solicitors
'Covid-19 and Criminal Law – The Essential Guide' by Ramya Nagesh
'Covid-19 and Family Law in England and Wales – The Essential Guide' by Safda Mahmood
'A Practical Guide to the Law of Unlawful Eviction and Harassment – 2nd Edition' by Stephanie Lovegrove
'Covid-19, Brexit and the Law of Commercial Leases – The Essential Guide' by Mark Shelton
'A Practical Guide to Costs in Personal Injury Claims – 2nd Edition' by Matthew Hoe

'A Practical Guide to the General Data Protection Regulation (GDPR) – 2nd Edition' by Keith Markham
'Ellis on Credit Hire – Sixth Edition' by Aidan Ellis & Tim Kevan
'A Practical Guide to Working with Litigants in Person and McKenzie Friends in Family Cases' by Stuart Barlow
'Protecting Unregistered Brands: A Practical Guide to the Law of Passing Off' by Lorna Brazell
'A Practical Guide to Secondary Liability and Joint Enterprise Post-Jogee' by Joanne Cecil & James Mehigan
'A Practical Guide to the Pre-Action RTA Claims Protocol for Personal Injury Lawyers' by Antonia Ford
'A Practical Guide to Neighbour Disputes and the Law' by Alexander Walsh
'A Practical Guide to Forfeiture of Leases' by Mark Shelton
'A Practical Guide to Coercive Control for Legal Practitioners and Victims' by Rachel Horman
'A Practical Guide to Rights Over Airspace and Subsoil' by Daniel Gatty
'Tackling Disclosure in the Criminal Courts – A Practitioner's Guide' by Narita Bahra QC & Don Ramble
'A Practical Guide to the Law of Driverless Cars – Second Edition' by Alex Glassbrook, Emma Northey & Scarlett Milligan
'A Practical Guide to TOLATA Claims' by Greg Williams
'A Practical Guide to Elderly Law – 2nd Edition' by Justin Patten
'A Practical Guide to Responding to Housing Disrepair and Unfitness Claims' by Iain Wightwick
'A Practical Guide to the Construction and Rectification of Wills and Trust Instruments' by Edward Hewitt
'A Practical Guide to the Law of Bullying and Harassment in the Workplace' by Philip Hyland
'How to Be a Freelance Solicitor: A Practical Guide to the SRA-Regulated Freelance Solicitor Model' by Paul Bennett
'A Practical Guide to Prison Injury Claims' by Malcolm Johnson
'A Practical Guide to the Small Claims Track - 2nd Edition' by Dominic Bright
'A Practical Guide to Advising Clients at the Police Station' by Colin Stephen McKeown-Beaumont
'A Practical Guide to Antisocial Behaviour Injunctions' by Iain Wightwick

'Practical Mediation: A Guide for Mediators, Advocates, Advisers, Lawyers, and Students in Civil, Commercial, Business, Property, Workplace, and Employment Cases' by Jonathan Dingle with John Sephton
'The Mini-Pupillage Workbook' by David Boyle
'A Practical Guide to Crofting Law' by Brian Inkster
'A Practical Guide to Spousal Maintenance' by Liz Cowell
'A Practical Guide to the Law of Domain Names and Cybersquatting' by Andrew Clemson
'A Practical Guide to the Law of Gender Pay Gap Reporting' by Harini Iyengar
'A Practical Guide to the Rights of Grandparents in Children Proceedings' by Stuart Barlow
'NHS Whistleblowing and the Law' by Joseph England
'Employment Law and the Gig Economy' by Nigel Mackay & Annie Powell
'A Practical Guide to Noise Induced Hearing Loss (NIHL) Claims' by Andrew Mckie, Ian Skeate, Gareth McAloon
'An Introduction to Beauty Negligence Claims – A Practical Guide for the Personal Injury Practitioner' by Greg Almond
'Intercompany Agreements for Transfer Pricing Compliance' by Paul Sutton
'Zen and the Art of Mediation' by Martin Plowman
'A Practical Guide to the SRA Principles, Individual and Law Firm Codes of Conduct 2019 – What Every Law Firm Needs to Know' by Paul Bennett
'A Practical Guide to Adoption for Family Lawyers' by Graham Pegg
'A Practical Guide to Industrial Disease Claims' by Andrew Mckie & Ian Skeate
'A Practical Guide to Redundancy' by Philip Hyland
'A Practical Guide to Vicarious Liability' by Mariel Irvine
'A Practical Guide to Applications for Landlord's Consent and Variation of Leases' by Mark Shelton
'A Practical Guide to Relief from Sanctions Post-Mitchell and Denton' by Peter Causton
'A Practical Guide to Equity Release for Advisors' by Paul Sams
'A Practical Guide to Financial Services Claims' by Chris Hegarty
'The Law of Houses in Multiple Occupation: A Practical Guide to HMO Proceedings' by Julian Hunt
'Occupiers, Highways and Defective Premises Claims: A Practical Guide Post-Jackson – 2nd Edition' by Andrew Mckie

www.ingramcontent.com/pod-product-compliance
Ingram Content Group UK Ltd.
Pitfield, Milton Keynes, MK11 3LW, UK
UKHW020150290926
15471UKWH00004B/785

9 781914 608223